Stand

A young Christian's guide to
the armour of God

Peter Jeffery

BRYNTIRION PRESS

© Peter Jeffery, 1983
First published 1983
Reprinted 1986, 1988, 1992, 1996, 1999

ISBN 0 900898 87 9

Cover design: burgum boorman ltd
Cover photograph: Gerallt Wyn Davies

Illustration of Roman Soldier by Mark Wójcicki

Published and typeset by the Bryntirion Press
Bryntirion, Bridgend CF31 4DX, Wales, UK
Printed by Interprint Ltd., Malta

Contents

A Roman soldier

'Finally, be strong in the Lord and in his mighty power. Put on the full armour of God so that you can take your stand against the devil's schemes. For our struggle is not against flesh and blood, but against the rulers, against the authorities, against the powers of this dark world and against the spiritual forces of evil in the heavenly realms. Therefore put on the full armour of God, so that when the day of evil comes, you may be able to stand your ground, and after you have done everything, to stand. Stand firm then, with the belt of truth buckled round your waist, with the breastplate of righteousness in place, and with your feet fitted with the readiness that comes from the gospel of peace. In addition to all this, take up the shield of faith, with which you can extinguish all the flaming arrows of the evil one. Take the helmet of salvation and the sword of the Spirit, which is the word of God. And pray in the Spirit on all occasions with all kinds of prayers and requests. With this in mind, be alert and always keep on praying for all the saints.'

(Ephesians 6:10-18)

Quotations are taken from the following publications:
J. M. Boice, *Does Inerrancy Matter?* (International Council on Biblical Inerrancy); Thomas Brooks, *Heaven on Earth* (Banner of Truth Trust); Matthew Henry, *Commentary on the Whole Bible* (Marshall, Morgan & Scott); Charles Hodge, *Commentary on Ephesians* (Banner of Truth Trust); D. M. Lloyd-Jones, *The Christian Soldier*, *The Christian Warfare*, and *The Final Perseverance of the Saints* (Banner of Truth Trust); J. I. Packer, 'Foreword', *Does Inerrancy Matter?* (see above), and *God's Words* (Inter-Varsity Press); Adolph Saphir —quoted in A. W. Pink, *An Exposition of Hebrews* (Baker Book House); J. C. Ryle, *Expository Thoughts on the Gospels —Matthew* and *Luke* (James Clarke, and also Evangelical Press); C. H. Spurgeon, *New Park Street Pulpit, 1859* (Banner of Truth Trust); A. W. Tozer, *That Incredible Christian* (STL Books).

Introduction

'Come to Jesus, and all your problems will be over' is the message we hear from some preachers. Certain hymns, too, seem to confirm this teaching—like the chorus that ends, 'And now I am happy all the day'. Unfortunately, however, that is not the Christian's experience after conversion and, more importantly, that is not what the Scriptures teach.

When a person comes to Christ in repentance and faith, sin—his greatest problem—is dealt with. The joy of salvation and the experience of peace with God can be overwhelming, and with some this may last for days, weeks or even months. But eventually other problems, completely unknown in pre-conversion days, will begin to make themselves felt. As a result, far from being 'happy all the day', the young Christian will know the misery of doubts, guilt and conviction of sin as never before. On top of all this, he will have to face misunderstanding and opposition to his new-found faith from friends and relatives.

All this can seem quite devastating to the new convert, but the Scriptures assure us that it is only to be expected. The Lord Jesus himself said to his disciples, 'In the world you will have trouble' (John 16:33). And the apostle Paul, returning to churches which he had established on his first missionary journey, to strengthen and encourage them, told them, 'We must go through many hardships to enter the kingdom of God' (Acts 14:22).

Why should it be like this? The fact is that when we become Christians, we enter not a holiday camp where everything is jolly and comfortable, but rather a battle station in the middle of a fierce war. We are now soldiers in the Lord's army, and the enemy exerts tremendous pressure upon us. How we fare in this spiritual battle depends to a great extent upon how we are equipped.

In Ephesians 6, verses 10-17, Paul teaches us about the armour that God has provided for his people: it is his equipment, his provision for us, and we must put it on. This book seeks to interpret that passage for young Christians, so as to help them to stand firm in their faith. But before reading any further, please read carefully chapters 1–3 of Ephesians.

The following chapters include a number of quotations from the writings of Dr Martyn Lloyd-Jones. I would earnestly advise you to read his two books, *The Christian Warfare* and *The Christian Soldier*, to which I am indebted for much of what follows.

Peter Jeffery

1
The enemy

'For our struggle is not against flesh and blood . . .'
(Ephesians 6:12)

Why is the Christian life such a battle? If God has done for us all that is described in the first three chapters of Ephesians, why do we struggle so much in the spiritual life, and why do we fail so often? The answer is given to us in Ephesians 6, verses 11, 12 and 16. We have an enemy, one who is at work with all his energies to pull us down. That enemy is the devil.

The devil is no ordinary enemy. His power and influence are awesome; his armies span the whole world. Even Jesus calls him 'the prince of this world' (John 14:30). Many people today dismiss the whole idea of the devil as medieval non-sense, but Jesus spoke of him as a real person. If we take the Bible seriously, then we must take the reality of the devil seriously too. The Bible teaches that he is not merely an evil influence, but a real person. He is as real as God. Who is he, then, and where does he come from?

Origin and power

The Bible uses several names for the enemy of souls. Some-times he is called the devil, sometimes Satan or Beelzebub or Belial. Originally his name was Lucifer (which means 'day star'), and he was an angel in heaven. We read of him in Isaiah

14. (The Authorised Version calls him 'Lucifer', the New International Version 'morning star'.) He was an angel who became ambitious and wanted to be greater than God (Isaiah 14:13-14). He was punished by God (verses 15-17) and expelled from heaven. Ever since, his one aim has been to disrupt and pollute all the works of God.

We see him first at work in the Garden of Eden (Genesis 3). By guile and temptation he caused Adam and Eve to rebel against the authority of God, as he himself had done. What happened then affected not only Adam and Eve, but every man, woman and child yet to be born. This is because, through Adam, sin became part of human nature (Romans 5:12-14) and, as a result, 'the whole world is under the control of the evil one' (1 John 5:19). The devil controls all mankind. He is the master, and we are born his children (John 8:44; 1 John 3:10).

It is men's sinfulness that accounts for the great hold the devil has upon them. He does not have to stand over his slaves with a whip to make them obey him. He merely lets the sin that is in them take its course, and that is enough. He is so cunning that he even allows his subjects to deny that he exists, but all the time his evil influence governs their lives. Sometimes he breaks out in obvious ways, and evil runs rampant. Either way, he rules in the lives of men and women.

God's answer

What is God's answer to this? The Lord Jesus gives it in a parable he told, which is recorded in Luke 11:21-22. The 'strong man, fully armed' is the devil; men and women are 'his possessions', and Jesus himself is the 'someone stronger'. At Calvary, God in Christ broke the devil's hold upon mankind. Read Colossians 2:13-15 and Hebrews 2:14-15. When we became Christians, not only were our sins forgiven, but the

10

lordship and control of Satan were broken. Jesus is now our Lord, and we are no longer slaves to sin (Romans 6:6-7).

This means that the devil no longer has any authority or control over the Christian. He cannot compel us to do anything. He can tempt, but temptation is not compulsion. Imagine a master with his slave. He owns the slave and can compel him to obey his every command. When he orders, 'Slave, dig a hole! Slave, feed the cattle! Slave, do this—go there!', the slave obeys, because he is a slave and has no freedom. But one day that slave dies. The master may still issue orders, but now there is no obedience. Why? The slave is dead and the master's power over him has ceased. This is what Paul means in Romans 6. The Christian is dead to sin (verse 11). Our old master, the devil, no longer has any authority over us. He cannot make us obey because Jesus has set us free. We are new creatures with a new master.

War

The devil does not take this lying down. He is defeated, and can never regain absolute power over the souls Jesus has saved. But he makes war on them and seeks to make their Christian life as difficult as possible. Before conversion we had little or no experience of the devil; we belonged to him, and so he did not need to attack us. But once salvation comes to a person, all hell erupts in anger and wages war on the new-born soul.

If you are a Christian, the devil is against you, and all the powers of hell are against you. It is a frightening prospect. What shall we do, then? Shall we cower in fear and give in? Shall we meekly surrender to every attack and temptation? No, most definitely not! Read 1 John 5:18 and see that the evil one cannot touch you. James 4:7 tells us, 'Resist the devil, and he will flee from you.' Martin Luther's great hymn rings with this confidence:

> *And were this world all devils o'er,*
> *And watching to devour us,*
> *We lay it not to heart so sore;*
> *Not they can overpower us.*
> *And let the prince of ill*
> *Look grim as e'er he will,*
> *He harms us not a whit:*
> *For why? his doom is writ;*
> *A word shall quickly slay him.*

What we must do is fight and get into the battle, realising that even though we have no strength of our own, we can still 'be strong in the Lord and in his mighty power' (Ephesians 6:10). The strength of the Lord has already proved to be too much for the powers of darkness. It is a trusted strength, a proved strength, and it is ours in Christ.

2
The enemy's strategy

*'Put on the full armour of God so that you can take
your stand against the devil's schemes.'*
(Ephesians 6:11)

History is full of battles, some of them short, and some long. But the battle in which we Christians are involved is not just a part of history; it is the whole of history. Everything that has happened in the history of mankind is directly or indirectly a part of this battle.

This battle is between God and Satan. Christ came into the world to get into the battle and to win it. The apostle John tells us that 'the whole world is under the control of the evil one', and that Jesus came into the world 'to destroy the devil's work' (1 John 5:19; 3:8).

From Bethlehem to Calvary the battle raged. When Jesus was born, Satan used his puppet, King Herod, to try and kill the Saviour. Satan failed, and Christ triumphed. At the beginning of Christ's public ministry Satan tried by a series of temptations to make the Saviour sin. Once more the evil one failed. The greatest conflict was on Calvary's cross. Charles Spurgeon, preaching on Colossians 2:15, creates for us this vivid picture:

Now must the Son of God arise, and gird His sword upon His thigh. Dread defeat or glorious conquest awaits the

Champion of the church. Which shall it be? We hold our breath with anxious suspense while the storm is raging . . . Satan came against Christ; he had in his hand a sharp sword called the Law, dipped in the poison of sin, so that every wound which the law inflicted was deadly. Christ dashed this sword out of Satan's hand, and there stood the prince of darkness unarmed. His helmet was cleft in twain, and his head was crushed as with a rod of iron. Death rose against Christ. The Saviour snatched his quiver from him, emptied out all his darts, cut them in two, gave Death back the feather end, but kept the poisoned barbs from him, that he might never destroy the ransomed. Sin came against Christ; but sin was utterly cut in pieces. It had been Satan's armour-bearer, but its shield was cast away, and it lay dead upon the plain. Is it not a noble picture to behold all the enemies of Christ?—nay, my brethren, all your enemies, and mine, totally disarmed? Satan has nothing left him now wherewith he may attack us. He may attempt to injure us, but wound us he never can, for his sword and spear are utterly taken away.

The final and complete victory of Christ is in the resurrection, where Satan's greatest weapons, death and the grave, are swallowed up in Christ's victory.

All this does not mean, however, that the battle is over. The ultimate victory is assured, but the fight still goes on. Christ is not now in the world in person; but the church is. The church is his body, consisting of his people, and so Satan now carries on the conflict against Christians. That is why we are in the battle.

When the apostle Paul was converted, God said that his ministry would be to turn sinners 'from the power of Satan to God' (Acts 26:18). This, partly, is the task of every believer,

14

and Satan is not going to take kindly to his doing this; he will oppose it with all his power. So the more we are involved in spiritual activities, the more we shall know the devil's opposition. You will know little of the battle when digging the garden or watching television or playing games; but the moment you get on your knees to pray, or open your Bible, or attempt to witness to an unbeliever, you will know that the battle is on.

Should we be depressed by this? No, because Ephesians 6:10 tells us that we are not on our own. It is the Lord's battle, and therefore he supplies us with his divine strength. We must never forget this. The armour is God's, and it is invincible. The battle is the Lord's, and he is almighty. But still we are in the battle, and we must prepare ourselves for the fight.

Recognise the enemy

The first thing to note is that we must learn to recognise the enemy. This battle is not like the old cowboy films, where all the 'baddies' wore black hats, and the 'goodies' white hats. Everything there was obvious and clear-cut. Our battle is not like that, because the devil does not fight that way. In Ephesians 6:11 Paul refers to the devil's 'schemes' or his 'wiles', and we are warned of this throughout Scripture. He is crafty (Genesis 3:1) and cunning (2 Corinthians 11:3); he will seek to outwit us (2 Corinthians 2:11) and set traps (1 Timothy 3:7); he is the master of lies (John 8:44) and can even perform miracles (Matthew 24:24).

You see, then, how careful the Christian has to be. The battle is not always obvious, and sometimes we can lose a skirmish before we are even aware that we are in it. We must therefore be continually on our guard. How often God's people are led into sin through something which seems innocent and harmless! This is due to the wiles and schemes of the devil.

The language the Bible uses to describe our enemy's activities is very expressive. Sometimes he 'prowls around like a roaring lion', and at other times 'masquerades as an angel of light' (1 Peter 5:8; 2 Corinthians 11:14). The 'angel of light' is far more dangerous than the 'prowling lion' because, whereas the one will put you on your guard, the other will take you unawares. In the Acts of the Apostles we see the devil as the roaring lion, stirring up his puppets to fierce and bitter persecution of the Christians. He still works like this, and will mount direct assaults upon us through various channels. The classic example of his coming as an angel of light we find in Genesis 3, when he comes to Eve full of apparent friendliness and concern, and yet craftily casts doubt on the truth of God's Word and character (verse 5).

The truth
When the enemy comes as an angel of light, it is the truth of God that exposes him for what he is. No matter how cleverly he masquerades, or how crafty his approach, the devil will always be in conflict with the truth of God as revealed in the Scriptures. God's Word is the searchlight that exposes the wiles of Satan.

Notice that twice in this passage in Ephesians 6 Paul refers to the truth of God. In verse 14 he speaks of 'the belt of truth', and in verse 17 of 'the sword of the Spirit, which is the word of God'. These parts of the armour of God are very important, because the enemy will never conform to the truth of God's Word. Everything in him rebels against the authority of God. Even though at times, when he wants to deceive us, he will try to give the impression that he is on God's side, once the searchlight of God's revealed truth is focused upon him, he is

16

seen for what he really is, the enemy of God.

The wiles of the devil are numerous, but perhaps the most prominent today can be grouped together under three headings: unholy alliances, false experiences, and false teaching. None of these things are new, but today they are particularly virulent.

Unholy alliances

To many people the work of the ecumenical movement and the idea of one church sound very attractive. Though Bible verses are sometimes quoted in support of it, unfortunately the general trend of the ecumenical movement shows little or no regard for biblical truth. The argument used is that doctrine and biblical teaching divide people, and therefore we must forget them; and the basic assumption made is that unity is more important than truth.

The question is, Is this of God or of the devil? The Bible says that it is *the truth* that alone unites us in Christ. Everywhere in his Word God stresses the importance of the truth. Worship, says Jesus, must be 'in spirit and in truth' (John 4:24). He goes even further and claims that he *is* the truth (John 14:6), and that it is the truth that sets men free from the bondage of sin (John 8:32).

Christian unity can only be based on the truth of God. To give the impression that 'oneness' is achieved simply through a common church organisation is wrong. These unholy alliances are one of the wiles of Satan which are exposed when God's Word is allowed to shine upon them (Romans 16:17-18; Titus 3:10; 2 Corinthians 6:14-18; Galatians 1:6-9; 2 John 7-11).

False experiences

There are many Christians today who claim to have had great experiences of the Spirit of God, and who talk excitedly of

17

signs and wonders. If these things are truly from God, then we should rejoice with them; but we must be careful, because the Bible warns us that the devil also can do signs and wonders (Matthew 24:24). We must never forget that it was not only Moses who turned sticks into snakes; Pharaoh's sorcerers did the same thing (Exodus 7:6-13).

A particularly dangerous offshoot of this is the claim these people sometimes make to having received direct revelation. 'God has told me to do it', they say. That may be so, but remember that God never contradicts himself. He will not tell us to do something that he has forbidden in Scripture. For example, a young man claimed that God had given him permission to sleep with his girlfriend. Did God do that, or is it a wile of the devil? The Word of God leaves us in no doubt as to who was behind it. You may perhaps argue that that is an extreme example. The application may be extreme, but the principle is not. To claim direct revelation from God without first examining it against the unchanging truth of God's Word is highly dangerous.

There are many Christians today who, because of this, are unteachable. They have put themselves *above* the authority of Scripture. We are told to stop being 'in bondage to the book', and we are urged 'to cut the apron strings of Mother Scripture and walk slowly but confidently over to the arms of our heavenly Father'. That is deadly advice. Our senses are still darkened by sin, and if we rely on them to lead us, we head towards error and leave ourselves open to the wiles of the devil.

False teaching
Whether the wiles of the devil take the form of unholy alliances or false experiences, in the end it all comes back to the influence of false teaching. The false teacher may be

18

genuine and sincere, but if what he teaches is contrary to the Word of God it is heresy. What we are taught and what we believe are of the utmost importance. Dr Martyn Lloyd-Jones says: 'One of the first things you are to learn in this Christian life and warfare is that, if you go wrong in your doctrine, you will go wrong in all aspects of your life. You will probably go wrong in your practice and behaviour; and you will certainly go wrong in your experience.'

It is therefore to be expected that Satan will use this particular ploy to attack us. It is not always easy to recognise a false teacher. If a man denies the deity of Jesus, or salvation by grace alone, or the resurrection, then it is obvious what he is. But Jesus warns us of wolves in sheep's clothing (Matthew 7:15). With these false teachers the problem is not so much what they say as what they do *not* say. In other words, they leave out much of the biblical gospel.

> What is the best safeguard against false teaching? Beyond all doubt the regular study of the Word of God, with prayer for the teaching of the Holy Spirit. The Bible was given to be a lamp to our feet and a light to our path (Psalm 119:105). The man who reads it aright will never be allowed greatly to err. It is neglect of the Bible which makes so many a prey to the first false teacher whom they hear . . . Happy is he who prays over his Bible, and knows the difference between truth and error in religion! There is a difference, and we are meant to know it, and to use our knowledge.
>
> *J. C. Ryle*

Pawns

Paul tells us that 'our struggle is not against flesh and blood' (Ephesians 6:12). This does not mean that, as Christians, we never find ourselves opposed by people. We have all had experiences of friends, workmates and family vigorously attacking our faith and beliefs. In his attacks upon us, the devil will use people as pawns, and it is not only unbelievers that he uses. There is great need for vigilance on our part, that we do not allow the enemy to use us to undermine the faith of fellow Christians, or to be a stumbling block to non-Christians. Our fight is not against flesh and blood, but the devil will use flesh and blood.

When we have to deal with sin and error, we must never forget the power behind it. Though we rightly hate the error taught, we must be very careful not to hate the people teaching it. To hate the sin and love the sinner is easier said than done, but it is crucial. Once we allow ourselves to be drawn away from the issues and to attack the personalities instead, we are in great danger of ourselves becoming pawns in the devil's hand.

3
Our strength

'Be strong in the Lord and in his mighty power.'
(Ephesians 6:10)

The battle is very real. It is fierce, and at times devious and very confusing. The more we think of it, the more we wonder how we can possibly survive, let alone triumph. It is easy to sympathise with Jehoshaphat, king of Judah, who, on the approach of a huge enemy army, came before God and said, 'O our God . . . we have no power to face this vast army . . . We do not know what to do' (2 Chronicles 20:12). But Jehoshaphat did not stop there; he went on to say, 'but our eyes are upon you'. His trust was in God, and the Lord rewarded that trust by telling him, 'the battle is not yours, but God's' (verse 15). He was encouraged to stand firm and not lose hope because he was assured that 'the LORD will be with you' (verse 17).

The battle is the Lord's, and we are only in it because we are his people. This does not mean that it is easy, or that all we have to do is stand aside and let God get on with it. God does not fight instead of us; *we* must fight, but in God's strength. The scriptural way is never 'Let go and let God', but rather 'Pray much and fight'. For every skirmish, for every trial, strength and power are supplied to us by God, but *we* must use it. Of course, there are times when God intervenes directly; those are most thrilling experiences, but they do not invalidate the main principle which he himself set down. The whole emphasis of this passage in Ephesians 6 is that it is God who supplies, but we who must use what he gives. How do we work this out in our lives?

Fight

Do not be afraid to get involved in the battle. The battle is unquestionably fierce, and you will get battered and bruised. Scars may well be left, but we must not be afraid of this. Some Christians hear the noise of battle; they see the casualties and they run. But that in itself is defeat. To let Satan march on unopposed is to deny our allegiance to Christ. Resist the devil, says James 4:7. Resist, not run. Whenever the enemy intrudes, confront him.

Notice that in Ephesians 6:12 Paul speaks of 'our struggle' —or, as the Authorised Version reads, 'we wrestle'. Wrestling involves personal contact—arms, legs and bodies entangled in confrontation. That is how the battle is. It is often a personal affair, with no one else involved. Satan attacks you, and you resist. This is spiritual wrestling.

Having said that we must resist and not run, it must also be said that sometimes the best way to resist *is* to run. This may appear contradictory, but it is not really so. To resist the devil, as we have seen, means to fight, not to give in and allow him to win. Now consider the following Scriptures:

1 Corinthians 6:18	'Flee from sexual immorality.'
1 Corinthians 10:14	'Flee from idolatry.'
1 Timothy 6:11	'Flee from all this.'
	(Read also verses 3-10.)
1 Timothy 2:22	'Flee the evil desires of youth.'

In all these passages, to 'flee' means to resist, to have nothing to do with these particular sins. Notice that the command to 'flee from all this' in 1 Timothy 6:11 is followed immediately by another, 'Fight the good fight of faith' (verse 12). These two commands really mean the same thing.

Remember

Remember who and what you are. You were once a slave to sin, but not any longer (Romans 6:6). You were once 'fast bound in sin and nature's night', but now the chains have fallen off and your heart is free. Now you are 'in Christ', and that means that you are 'more than conqueror' (Romans 8:37). Your strength is derived from Christ. It is only through him that you became a conqueror; in and of yourself you are no match for Satan. Can you imagine yourself in a boxing ring facing the heavyweight champion of the world? The situation would be hopeless. But what if you were facing the same champion, only that you were in a Centurion tank? You are still the same weakling compared to your opponent, but now the situation is not hopeless. You have a strength and invincibility that comes from being in the tank.

This is nothing compared to what it means to be 'in Christ'. In him you are more than a conqueror.

Know God

'The people who know their God will firmly resist [the enemy]' (Daniel 11:32). Here is your greatest strength. The more we know God, the stronger we are for the battle. James tells us, 'Resist the devil, and he will flee from you' (James 4:7). Look this verse up, and notice that immediately before these encouraging words we are told, 'Submit yourselves, then, to God,' and immediately afterwards, 'Come near to God'.

It is only as we submit to God's will, draw near to him, and know him in all his beauty and wonder, that we are able to gain victory in the battle. This was David's strength when he faced Goliath (1 Samuel 17:37,45-47). The apostles faced a bitterly hostile world that sought to destroy their faith, and it was their real and continuing awareness of God's presence that sustained them (Acts 4:19,31). This same awareness of God with us is our only hope in facing the devil.

In order to bring out this point let me tell you the story of a quaint old preacher preaching on this very text ['I can do all things through Christ which strengtheneth me' (Philippians 4:13 AV)]. In order to impress the point upon his congregation he put it like this. He read the words, 'I can do all things'—then stopped abruptly and put a ques-tion to the Apostle in these words: 'Don't you think you are saying too much, Paul? Do you really say you can do all things? Is there nothing that you cannot do? Can you really fight these principalities and powers? Are you equal to the devil? Look what he did with all the patriarchs, even men like Abraham, the friend of God. The devil defeated Abraham, and are you claiming that you are superior when you say "I can do all things"?' The old preacher went on in that man-ner for some time, putting up the difficulties and asking the Apostle questions and suggesting that Paul was going beyond himself. But then he proceeded to read the whole text, 'I can do all things through Christ which strengtheneth me.' 'Oh, I beg your pardon, Paul,' said the old preacher, 'I didn't realize that there were two of you!' He had been giv-ing the impression that there was only one, namely, the Apostle Paul. Certainly that must be empha-sized: 'I', says Paul, 'can do all things'. But he is able to do all things only

24

'through Christ which strengtheneth me'. Christ is strengthening him, is infusing power into him; but it is Paul who does all things. It is he who knows both how to be abased, and how to abound. Paul has not handed it all over and become a sitting spectator passively 'abiding'. He is involved, he is the one who is doing all these things. But the glory of it is, he says, that I am enabled to do all these things through Christ who—not, 'does it all for me', but Christ who—'strengtheneth me'. It is a kind of blood transfusion, the power is put into him, he is strengthened. The tasks are not taken out of his hands, but he is enabled to do them because he is being strengthened in this way.

D. M. Lloyd-Jones

God supplies both the armour and the strength, and this he does for every Christian. Why, then, if we all have the same resources, do some Christians fight the fight of faith and triumph, while others hardly fight at all and, when they do, melt like chocolate soldiers in the heat of battle? The answer is that, apart from anything else, the soldier needs two essential qualities: discipline and endurance.

Discipline

The armour is available, but it has to be put on. It will not put itself on, and God will not put it on for us. Paul is very definite in Ephesians 6:11, and again in verse 13. The command is clear and crisp: 'Put on the full armour of God.' This is a matter of discipline and, of course, of obedience.

No army can function without discipline. Battles are won and lost not so much by great deeds of bravery on the part of one or two, but by the planning and strategy of the generals and the discipline of the soldiers in carrying them out. Consequently, almost the first thing a recruit is taught when he joins the army is discipline. In basic training he will spend a great deal of time learning to obey. Hours are spent on the parade square in what is known as 'square-bashing'. Quick march, right turn, left turn, about turn, slope arms, present arms, order arms—the commands come quick and fast, until they are obeyed without hesitation. In any war, discipline can be a matter of life and death. During the Second World War, the warning siren sounded when enemy planes were approaching, and the discipline of reacting immediately by rushing to the air-raid shelter saved many lives. The same dis-cipline caused everyone to carry a gas mask at all times. If there were an attack of gas bombs, what use would this pro-tection be if you did not have it with you?

If this is true when fighting flesh and blood, how much more so when fighting the enemy described in verse 12! Paul tells Timothy that without discipline there is no hope of victory (1 Timothy 4:7-8). He urges him, 'train yourself to be godly'. Are you doing that? The athlete in his physical training needs a great deal of discipline, and so does the Christian, both in preparing for the battle and indeed throughout the battle. The Christian needs to be disciplined in the following areas:

- *Discipline in the use of time.* How much of our time is wasted, and how much time we give to trivial things rather than to spiritual exercises!

- *Discipline in prayer.* Prayer is not easy, and therefore many Christians pray little. Yet this is one of the most precious of God's gifts to us. Prayer is the hottest place in the battle, and when you pray the devil comes strongly to disturb you. Not to give in, therefore, requires discipline and persever-ance. Some believers do not understand this. They think that prayer should always be easy, so if it is difficult they leave it. That is the devil's advice. God's Word says that we are to wrestle, labour and strive in prayer; it is a very important part of the battle.

Is your prayer life disciplined? Do you give time and effort to it? And what about your church's prayer meeting? Because it is often hard, have you stopped attending? That, again, is Satan's advice. God tells us to pray. Pray on your own, and pray with other Christians.

• *Discipline in Bible study.* The first part of the armour is truth. How do we know the truth? Only by reading and studying God's Word. Reading the Bible is not enough; we must give time to study it. 'Do your best to present yourself to God as one approved, a workman who does not need to be ashamed and who correctly handles the word of truth' (2 Timothy 2:15).

The armour has to be put on, and this is how we do it—with discipline and obedience. When you get out of bed in the morning, how do you put your clothes on? Do you stand there like some spiritual Mary Poppins waiting for everything to float into its appointed place? Of course not! You have to put on the various garments. So too it is with God's armour—you must put it on.

Endurance

When we have put on the whole armour we are able to stand firm and endure, and we will then be able to cope with all that the enemy throws at us. Paul encourages Timothy to do this: 'Endure hardship with us like a good soldier of Christ Jesus' (2 Timothy 2:3). Endurance means staying power. Many Christians start off on their spiritual pilgrimage fizzing like a bottle of pop, but sadly, all too soon, they are flat like a bottle of water. Why was there no endurance, no standing firm? The probable answer is that they failed to put on the *whole* armour of God.

If you ever visit Windsor Castle, you will be able to see Henry VIII's armour. He was a big man, and he had a complete suit of armour specially made for him. The claim was that while he was wearing this he was invulnerable. Could you imagine Henry VIII charging into battle with his helmet on and carrying his shield and sword, but still wearing his nightgown? Of course not; that would be ridiculous.

Yet many Christians do exactly that. You will not stand simply because you are saved; neither will you stand merely by taking a great interest in the truth, or in faith, or in prayer. You need them *ALL*: not truth *or* faith *or* prayer, but truth *and* faith *and* prayer. There are Christians who are unshakeable on the truth of Scripture, but they are not much use as soldiers of the Lord because they do not know the true place and value of prayer. The opposite can also be true. It is possible to put a strong emphasis on prayer and give much time to it, and yet to accomplish little or nothing in the battle. The reason for this is that, because such people neglect Scripture, they are easily deceived by the wiles of Satan. The only way to endure is with the whole armour on.

Our strength comes from God, and we need the armour he provides.

4
The belt of truth

'Stand firm then, with the belt of truth
buckled round your waist.'
(Ephesians 6:14)

The finest soldiers of Paul's time were undoubtedly the men of the Roman legions; they had conquered virtually all the known world. In his journeys the apostle had seen these soldiers at close quarters on several occasions (Acts 12:30-37; 23:23-24). He was therefore very familiar with their equipment, and in Ephesians 6 he uses this to illustrate the equipment available to the Christian soldier for the spiritual battle. There are six pieces of equipment mentioned here. Nothing in Paul's teaching is ever haphazard. When he makes a list, the order of things is generally important, and this is certainly the case with the armour of God.

We start first with the *belt of truth* buckled round the waist. What is the function of this belt? In the first century a man wore long, flowing garments—something like an old-fashioned nightgown. To try and run or fight in something like that would be impossible. The man would be tripping over it; he would never feel secure on his feet, and this would have obvious dangers. So he was equipped with a belt, its purpose being to hitch up and bind together the long, flowing robes, thus leaving the man free for action.

It becomes clear, then, why this piece of equipment is

mentioned first: it means being ready for action. You may have all the other parts of the armour, but if you are not ready, not prepared, then you will be caught unawares.

What has this to do with our spiritual battle against the devil? Paul is arguing that *truth* is the first essential, and it is on this that the usefulness and effectiveness of everything else depends. Some people think that the word 'truth' here means truthfulness or sincerity. That cannot be its meaning, because truthfulness or sincerity is something we produce ourselves, whereas every part of this armour is provided for us by God.

If in battle we are to rely primarily upon our own sincerity, then we are certainly doomed to failure. No, what 'truth' means here is a knowledge and belief of the truth. This is the first and indispensable qualification of the soldier of the Lord. To face the enemy with a mind filled with confusion and doubt is to be a spiritual cripple before a mighty foe.

As the girdle [or belt] gives strength and freedom of action, and therefore confidence, so does the truth when spiritually apprehended and believed. Let not any one imagine that he is prepared to withstand the assaults of the powers of darkness, if his mind is stored with his own theories or with the speculations of other men. Nothing but the truth of God clearly understood and cordially embraced will enable him to keep his feet for a moment, before these celestial potentates. Reason, tradition, speculative conviction, dead orthodoxy, are a girdle of spider-webs. They give way at the first onset. Truth alone, as abiding in the mind in the form of divine knowledge, can give strength or confidence even in the ordinary conflicts of the Christian life, much more in any really 'evil day'.

Charles Hodge

The belt signifies unqualified confidence in the truth of Scripture. This is the foundation of everything. Later on in the passage (verse 17), Paul deals with the matter of how to use this truth, but here it is the truth itself that he brings before us.

The Bible and science

Jesus tells us that God's Word is truth (John 17:17). It is essential to believe this, and that is why the devil spends so much time trying to discredit the Scriptures. There is nothing new about this. Ever since the church was born, Satan has been attacking it in this way. In the second century, a very earnest and sincere man named Marcion came to prominence in Christianity; but he rejected all the Old Testament and most of the New Testament, with the exception of ten of Paul's epistles and the Gospel of Luke. He even edited these to suit his own particular doctrines.

The attack on the Word of God intensified in the twentieth century with the growth of the Bible-versus-science controversy, and this has caused some Christians to lose confidence in the truth of the Scriptures. But there is no need for this. Science can never disprove the Bible. The trouble is that, very often, what science tenaciously believes today it will cheerfully reject tomorrow, on the grounds that it has now been disproved by new scientific 'truths'. For instance, Christians claim that Moses wrote the first five books of the Bible. At one time science said that was impossible, because writing had not been invented in Moses' time. Since then, however, archaeologists have discovered thousands of inscriptions dating back long before the time of Moses, and it is now known that in his day there were at least six different written languages.

The results of scholarship, far from discrediting the Bible,

31

actually support its truthfulness. Of course, they do not prove inerrancy. We will probably never have all the data that would be necessary to do that. But they do point in the direction of reliability and reveal nothing that is not compatible with the highest view of Scripture. Even *Time* magazine acknowledged this in a cover story on the Bible (December 30, 1974): 'After more than two centuries of facing the heaviest scientific guns that could be brought to bear, the Bible has survived—and is perhaps the better for the siege. Even on the critics' own terms—historical fact—the Scriptures seem more acceptable now than they did when the rationalists began the attack.'

No Christian should ever fear to stand upon the Word of God. At times theories will challenge it. The arguments may seem unanswerable, and the one who stands by the Bible will be called foolish. The wise of the world will say, 'You can believe that nonsense if you want to, but science teaches us better.' This has happened before and will happen again. But the Christian who will stand upon Scripture will find even within his lifetime that, as the so-called 'assured results' begin to crumble about the scholars, the view of the Bible held by the Lord Jesus Christ and the historical Christian church will prevail.

James Montgomery Boice

Authority

The 'belt of truth' settles for us what our authority is. This is of crucial importance because of the nature of the battle and the character of the enemy. The devil is 'a liar and the father of lies' (John 8:44), and the only way to combat lies is with truth. But what is truth? Jesus said, 'your word is truth' (John 17:17). The Bible therefore is our only authority. There are many excellent books available today to help us understand more of God: books to encourage, guide and instruct; books written by spiritual men whose only motive is to glorify God and help his people. But none of these books is infallible, and so they cannot be our final authority. Only the Bible is the infallible Word of the infallible God. The Bible is not the word of man:

'Above all, you must understand that no prophecy of Scripture came about by the prophet's own interpretation. For prophecy never had its origin in the will of man, but men spoke from God as they were carried along by the Holy Spirit' (2 Peter 1:20-21).

The Bible is inspired by God:

'All Scripture is God-breathed [inspired]' (2 Timothy 3:16).

It is because of this that we can rely upon it as our infallible authority in the spiritual battle. How do we know what to believe, or how can we be sure of what is right or wrong? We turn to Scripture and ask, What does God's Word say? The Bible is to be a lamp to our feet and a light for our path (Psalm 119:105): in other words, it is our final authority.

It is vital for our survival in the battle that we settle once and for all in our minds the question of biblical authority and inerrancy. Dr. James Packer tells us:

I assert biblical *inerrancy*, and encourage all faithful Christians to do the same.

For, first, it is *true*. If, as Christ and Paul among others believed, Scripture 'came through the instrumentality of men from the very mouth of God' (Calvin), any idea of it teaching and affirming some falsehoods must be dismissed as blasphemous nonsense.

33

Second, it is *clarifying*. He who asserts inerrancy thereby shows what he means when he calls Scripture inspired, authoritative and infallible. We owe such honesty to each other.

Third, it is *health-giving* ('sound doctrine' in the New Testament sense), for it leads to that systematic submission of our proud minds to Scripture without which we cannot but lose some of God's precious truth.

Put on

We put on the belt of truth when we have an unqualified confidence in the truth of the Word of God. When our beliefs and doctrines are governed exclusively by the Bible, and not by reasoning or by feeling or by what men say, then we are wearing the belt of truth. When our standard of behaviour is determined solely by the Scriptures, and not by current social standards or what is convenient or easy, then the belt of truth is firmly in place.

If we do not put on the belt of truth, we shall never be victorious soldiers. We may talk about faith or we may pray as much as we like, but the devil will defeat us every time. The advice of the Lord to Joshua is still very relevant to us today:

'Do not let this book of the Law depart from your mouth; meditate on it day and night, so that you may be careful to do everything written in it. Then you will be prosperous and successful. Have I not commanded you? Be strong and courageous. Do not be terrified; do not be discouraged, for the Lord your God will be with you wherever you go' (Joshua 1:8-9).

5

The breastplate of righteousness

'with the breastplate of righteousness in place'
(Ephesians 6:14)

The breastplate was a piece of armour that covered the body from the neck to the thighs. It consisted of two parts, front and back. Without the protection of the breastplate no soldier would last very long in the battle; any spear-thrust or stray arrow could kill him instantly. It was this piece of armour that protected the heart and other vital parts of the body.

We need something to protect the heart in our spiritual warfare, because the devil is always attacking this vital part of the Christian. In biblical language, the heart is regarded as the centre of our desires. Our feelings, emotions, conscience, affections and will are all included in the protection offered by the breastplate of righteousness. Every believer knows attacks in these areas. How often we are governed by our feelings, going up and down emotionally like yo-yos! It is the same with our desires. One day we hunger after the things of God, and the next we are dominated by worldly pleasures and desires. All this is very real, and it cannot always be explained merely in terms of temperament; it is the devil attacking us. It is crucial therefore to wear the protective armour and to use

the spiritual resources that God provides to enable us to fight
and triumph at this point.

Righteousness
What does 'righteousness' mean here? In our interpretation of
these words we must never forget that it is *God*'s armour, not
ours. Therefore this righteousness is not ours. Paul is referring
not to our integrity and moral character, but to God's righteousness. To enter the battle dressed in our own righteousness
would put us in a hopeless position; such armour would be
much too flimsy. The devil loves to see Christians dress in it,
for it makes his evil task much easier. What we need is God's
armour, God's righteousness.

If we enter the battle relying upon our own righteousness—
that is, feeling confident in how good we are, how spiritual,
how prayerful, how knowledgeable in the Scriptures—then
the devil will challenge us by revealing areas in our lives of
which we are not so proud. He will point out areas where self
still reigns and Christ is excluded. He will show us other
Christians who are so much more sanctified than we are, and
whose lives make ours look positively tarnished. By this type
of attack our righteousness is easily demolished and we are
left defenceless.

What we need is a righteousness that is invulnerable, and this
is exactly what God provides. In Philippians 3:9, Paul writes of
being found in Christ, 'not having a righteousness of my own
that comes from the law, but that which is through faith in
Christ—the righteousness that comes from God and is by faith'.
If you read the previous verses (4-6) you will see that at one
time Paul trusted a great deal in his own righteousness. But now
that he was a Christian, he realised that all that was rubbish
(verse 8) compared to the righteousness that God provides.

Imputed

When we became Christians, God covered us in the righteousness of Christ (Romans 3:21-22; 5:17; 10:3-11). In the Authorised Version of the Bible this righteousness is described as 'imputed', and in the New International Version as 'credited'. Read Romans 4:18-25.

> This is the thought expressed by the traditional phrase 'the imputation of Christ's righteousness'—namely, that believers are righteous (Rom. 5:19) and have righteousness (Phil. 3:9) in God's sight (Rom. 4:11), not because they are righteous in themselves, but because Christ their Head was righteous before God and they are one with Him, sharers of His status and acceptance. His righteousness becomes theirs in the sense that they are accepted and rewarded as His righteousness, His full obedience to the Father, deserves to be. The imputing of His righteousness to them in this sense is not an arbitrary legal fiction, as is sometimes alleged, for it is grounded on a real union between themselves and Him. They are justified 'in Christ' (Gal. 2:17); and God reckons them righteous and declares them so, not because He accounts them to have kept His law personally (which would be a false judgement), but because He accounts them to be united by faith to the One who kept it representatively (and that is a true judgement).
>
> *J. I. Packer*

Isaiah has a lovely picture of this: 'I delight greatly in the Lord; my soul rejoices in my God. For he has clothed me with garments of salvation and arrayed me in a robe of righteousness' (Isaiah 61:10). Before we became Christians, how delighted we were with our own righteousness! How proud we were of our efforts! We thought, 'I am as good as anyone. Who can tell me I am a sinner?' The robe of self-righteousness fitted well and we loved it, until God showed us the perfect, sinless purity of Jesus and said, 'all our righteous acts are like filthy rags' (Isaiah 64:6). Before long we too saw them as filthy rags, and we felt guilty and convicted of sin. Our problem then was, Where could we find another robe to replace our discredited robe of self-righteousness? God answered, 'Come to me and I will clothe you in the garment of salvation.' When we came to God in repentance and faith, what did we find? Not a judge to condemn us, not one to mock our efforts and shame us in our guilt, but a loving heavenly Father, full of grace and compassion and mercy. He took us to his wardrobe of sovereign grace and brought out the robe of righteousness. We saw the price tag—'purchased by the blood of Jesus'—and we noticed in amazement that it already had our name on it. It was fitted by the Holy Spirit, and was perfect. Then, like Isaiah, we 'delighted greatly in the Lord' and rejoiced.

All that happened when we were saved. Righteousness was imputed (or credited) to us. Why did a soldier put on a breastplate when going into battle? Though he might have been strong as an ox and superbly fit, he realised that, for all that, his natural body could not withstand a spear, sword or arrow. So he covered himself with another body, a much stronger one —a breastplate. His protection then was not *in* him but *upon* him. In the same way our breastplate, our protection, is the imputed righteousness of God.

Imparted
Thank God for imputed righteousness, but it is not an end in itself. There is also 'imparted' righteousness. Having been

saved by grace and covered with the imputed righteousness of God, the Holy Spirit of God now begins to work within us to change or to sanctify us. Gradually our thinking, our desires and our outlook on life all begin to change. We will never be sinless in this world, but we find ourselves beginning to hate sin. What is happening? This is 'imparted righteousness'. The righteousness which in our salvation was not ours, but covered us like a robe, is now becoming a part of us. We begin to grow in grace and a knowledge of God.

The difference between imputed righteousness and imparted righteousness is that imputed righteousness is all Christ's and is perfect and absolute. It covers us and makes us acceptable to God. Imparted righteousness is the Holy Spirit making us more like Jesus. It is the continual work of God within us, and whilst in this life it will never make us perfect, it does make us more Christlike. It is this imparted righteousness that makes us hate all that the devil stands for. We are new creatures with a new Lord and Master, and we fight evil.

This, then is the breastplate of righteousness that is going to protect our heart and all that flows from it—our feelings, desires, conscience. It is the righteousness of God, which was imputed to us in salvation and is gradually being imparted to us in the inward work of the Holy Spirit.

Assurance
When a soldier entered battle wearing his breastplate, he had a great sense of confidence and assurance; he knew he had protection.

> The breastplate of righteousness helps us in the first place by giving us a general sense of confidence, and this is always essential to our warfare. If you enter into this fight

with the devil uncertainly or hesitantly you are already defeated. We need confidence. Here I stand, as it were, as a soldier, and I know something about the enemy. I have examined his dispositions, I have discovered something about the powers that he commands, and the armaments that he is able to use, and I know that they are characterized by subtlety and by power and by strength. I am also aware of these sensitive organs within me which are exposed to his attack. Until I have a feeling of confidence that they are covered I cannot possibly stand and be ready for some particular onslaught that is coming. But the moment I have this breastplate I know that all is well. In a sense this means, therefore, assurance of salvation; a realization of our whole position and standing.

D. M. Lloyd-Jones

Assurance of salvation is one of the most valuable assets for the Christian soldier in his fight against the devil, and it is God's will for all his people (Hebrews 10:22; 1 John 5:13; Romans 8:16). It is not surprising therefore that Satan is always attempting to sow doubts in our minds.

Satan knows . . . that assurance is that which will make men strong to do exploits, to shake his tottering kingdom about his ears; and therefore he is very studious and industrious to keep souls off from assurance.

Thomas Brooks

Feelings

Assurance can become vulnerable at this point of our feelings. Feelings are a very important part of each one of us, especially in our spiritual life. You cannot really believe the gospel without feeling something. A man who claims to believe the gospel of God's grace, and yet is unmoved by it, is either not saved or

40

in a serious condition of spiritual backsliding. No one can be in the presence of God and remain unmoved; feelings and emotion are inevitable. Turn to Isaiah 6 and see the depth of the prophet's feeling in the presence of God: 'Woe to me!' (verse 5). Similarly, in Acts 5 we find the early Christians responding with 'great fear' (verse 5) and 'rejoicing' (verse 41).

All this is perfectly normal, but the devil seeks to make us attach too much importance to feelings. Feelings can excite, stimulate, and encourage, but the trouble is that they never last. Sooner or later they will go. The sense of joy and exhilaration you felt in the Sunday services has very often departed by the time you get to work on Monday morning. This is why feelings can be extremely dangerous and are notoriously unreliable. For instance, it is not sufficient to say, 'I know God loves me because I feel it in my heart.' What about the times when you don't feel it in your heart?

If we rely too much on our feelings, this is what will happen. At times when our feelings are not so strong as we think they ought to be, the devil will pour into our minds all sorts of doubts as to whether or not we are true believers, and as a result depression and despondency will flood our souls. The trouble with many Christians is that they *feel* too much and *think* too little. And it is these Christians who are troubled most with lack of assurance. Have you ever noticed that the very believers who can experience great heights of ecstatic spiritual joy can also know depths of utter despair? The reason is that the feelings that lift them and so enrich their spiritual life can also, if left unchecked, lay them low and greatly impoverish their souls.

Feelings are important—and if you do not have any, beware!—but never base your faith and life upon them. That is one of the wiles of the devil. Our faith is not dependent upon our feelings, but upon the love and grace of God to us in Christ. Our confidence is in the imputed righteousness of God. That is what it means to put on the breastplate of righteousness. Our assurance is in what God has done for us once and for all, and not in the particular feelings of the moment.

There is a story told of two Hebrew boys on the night of the Passover (Exodus 12). Each was the eldest in his family and knew that the pronouncement of God (verse 12) included him. Their only hope was in the promise of God (verse 13), that if the blood of the passover lamb was sprinkled on the door frame of their home, then the judgement would pass over them. Their families did as God commanded and the two boys went to bed on that fateful night. One slept without any trouble, confident that he was safe under the blood. The other tossed and turned all night, worrying about the outcome. The question is asked, Which of those two boys was the safer? One trusted, while the other was plagued with feelings of worry and uncertainty; yet each was as safe as the other. Their safety did not depend upon their feelings, but on the word of God that 'when I see the blood, I will pass over you'.

Conscience
The devil also attacks us in our conscience. He is called in Scripture 'the accuser' (Revelation 12:10). He brings our sin before us constantly and accuses us with it, saying such things as: 'You young men who call yourselves Christians, what about your thoughts of those girls? You young women who call yourselves Christians, what about your vanity and envy and gossip? You older men and women who call yourselves Christians, what about your greed and materialism and worldliness?'

In these and other ways he accuses us of not being true

42

Christians. We all know something of this, and feel our consciences smitten and bruised. What do we do? Here again is the value of the breastplate. You flee to the righteousness of Christ.

> *What though th' accuser roar*
> *Of ills that I have done?*
> *I know them well, and thousands more:*
> *Jehovah findeth none.*
>
> S. W. Gandy

That is the glory of imputed righteousness and justification by faith. That is what it means to put on the breastplate of righteousness.

> *When Satan tempts me to despair,*
> *And tells me of the guilt within,*
> *Upward I look, and see Him there*
> *Who made an end of all my sin.*
>
> *Because the sinless Saviour died,*
> *My sinful soul is counted free;*
> *For God the Just is satisfied*
> *To look on Him, and pardon me.*
>
> Charitie Lees De Chenez

The breastplate is invulnerable, because the devil has no answer to the atoning death of Christ. His righteousness is our strength and defence.

Put on

We put on the breastplate of righteousness when we are absolutely dependent upon the Lord Jesus Christ and his righteousness. We must therefore learn to glory in Christ, to magnify him and to delight in him. It is this that causes Satan to flee. If you keep on trusting in your own abilities and depending upon good feelings, you will always have Satan sitting on your shoulder and gloating at his success.

Imputed righteousness assures us that our sins have been dealt with. Imparted righteousness guards us from treating sin lightly, and will create in us a hatred of the devil and his works. Imputed and imparted righteousness combine in the breastplate, and together they form God's provision to protect us against the accusations and insinuations of the enemy.

> *Though sin would fill me with distress,*
> *The throne of grace I dare address,*
> *For Jesus is my righteousness.*
>
> *Against me earth and hell combine;*
> *But on my side is power divine;*
> *Jesus is all, and He is mine!*
>> John Newton

6
The gospel of peace

'and with your feet fitted with the readiness that
comes from the gospel of peace'
(Ephesians 6:15)

Since ancient warfare was fought mainly by hand-to-hand combat, sureness of foot was one of the most important qualities in a soldier. This is what Paul is referring to when he says, 'Stand firm . . . with your feet fitted with the readiness that comes from the gospel of peace.' The Roman soldier's footwear could perhaps best be described as hob-nailed sandals. Josephus the historian called them 'shoes thickly studded with sharp nails'. This was unusual in those days and it gave them a great advantage over the enemy.

Thus, one important reason for Julius Caesar's success as a general was the fact that his men wore military shoes that made it possible for them to cover long distances in such short periods that again and again the enemies were caught off guard, having deceived themselves into thinking that they still had plenty of time to prepare an adequate defence. In the victories won by Alexander the Great this same factor had played an important role.

William Hendriksen

These special shoes gave the Roman soldier a firm footing, so that he would not slide around unsteadily if fighting on slippery ground. It also gave him great mobility. The combination of these two factors—stability and mobility—increased his sense of readiness, and his zeal and confidence for battle. The apostle Paul says that as *we* enter the battle, the gospel of peace should produce these same things in us.

Peace
The peace which the gospel produces is 'peace with God' (Romans 5:1). This must never be confused with peace of mind. All men are looking for peace of mind: some seek it in drugs, some in drink, and others in more creative forms of pleasure. The world is a miserable place and in turmoil, so it is not surprising that people want peace of mind. False religions and so-called 'Christian' cults pander to this desire and produce an easy 'salvation'. 'Come our way,' they say, 'and have no worries. Forget your troubles and have peace.' Many people fall for this and find some sort of peace; but it is not peace with God. The Bible knows of no peace with God that bypasses the question of man's sin and guilt. More than that, the Bible exposes and warns people of the false peace produced by the preachers of easy religion (Ezekiel 13).

There is a peace, then, which is not peace with God. What are the marks of this false peace? They are these: no repentance, no sense of the awfulness of sin, no battle with sin, no striving. These things are absent because this sort of peace is psychological, not spiritual.

True peace with God is the product of the gospel, because it is the gospel alone that deals with our sin and guilt before a holy God. When a man becomes a Christian, this glorious peace becomes his real experience. But there is a paradox here, because the moment we become Christians we are also involved in warfare, and this too is a very real experience. Peace and

46

warfare, both at the same time—how can this be possible?

Peace in battle *is* possible for the Christian, because in this warfare there are three crucial factors, which sum up how worth while it is. They are (1) the nobility of the cause; (2) the certainty of victory, and (3) the glory awaiting the victors.

The cause is the glory of God on earth and the vanquishing of sin and evil. The certain victory, and the glory awaiting the victors, are alike assured by the death and resurrection of our Lord Jesus Christ. With this knowledge we can not only enter the battle at peace *with* God, but also with the peace *of* God filling our hearts and minds.

Stability

In Ephesians 4:14, the apostle Paul expresses the longing that Christians should 'no longer be infants, tossed back and forth by the waves, and blown here and there by every wind of teaching and by the cunning and craftiness of men in their deceitful scheming'. There we have a perfect picture of spiritual instability. Inevitably the matter of stability is a problem that faces every new convert. He has only recently been converted; he is born again and is now a babe in Christ. Like all babes, he may be able to make a lot of noise, but he is not very firm on his feet; he has no stability. It is therefore of prime importance to attain spiritual stability as soon as possible.

It is a sad fact that too many believers, even though they have been converted for many years, are still spiritual infants. They are 'blown here and there by every wind of teaching'. They eagerly lap up every latest spiritual trend or emphasis, and consequently they are useless in the battle. They cannot take their stand on the truth of the gospel because they are never sure what it is. They slide about all over the place; they hold strange views, do strange things and are completely

47

inconsistent. Why? Because their feet are not 'fitted with the readiness that comes from the gospel of peace'. They have never been interested in Bible teaching and doctrine. Like the typical infant, what they want is something to play with, something to entertain them, something sweet to the taste and pleasant to the eye. The result after many years is spiritual infancy and instability.

If you are a new convert, don't make these mistakes. The only way to avoid them is to put on this particular part of the armour. It is the gospel that gives us peace with God, and therefore it is the gospel that will alone enable us to stand firm. The gospel does not consist of some vague, undefined thoughts; it is the clear, unchanging word of the living God. What it says it means, and we must believe it.

Spiritual stability comes from an unswerving confidence in what God has said. We must know what we believe and stand firm on it. Martin Luther, the Reformer, is a great example to us here. When in 1521 he was brought before the might of the Roman Catholic Church to answer for his faith, he replied:

> Since then Your Majesty and your lordships require from me a clear, simple, and precise answer, I will give you one, and it is this: I cannot submit my faith either to the pope or to the councils, because it is clear as the day that they have frequently erred and contradicted each other. Unless therefore I am convinced by the testimony of Scripture, or by the clearest reasoning—unless I am persuaded by means of the passages I have quoted—and unless they thus render my conscience bound by the Word of God, I cannot and I will not retract, for it is unsafe for a Christian to speak against his conscience.

Luther was in great danger of losing his life. Yet, facing the

Emperor Charles V and a host of political and religious leaders, he boldly declared, 'Here I stand. I cannot do otherwise. May God help me! Amen.' Even the Emperor was forced to say, 'The monk speaks with an intrepid heart and unshaken courage.'

Martin Luther's stability was the result of his study of Scripture and his closeness to God. He knew what he believed and why he believed it. Though we shall probably never attain to the same spiritual knowledge and strength as Martin Luther, God requires us all to attain spiritual stability. The way to this, first and foremost, is to know God's Word. This means study, and more study. There is no substitute for this.

Thinking and applying

But it does not end there. We must also learn to apply God's Word to our lives. Sometimes Christians are heard to complain that there is not enough application in the sermons they hear. This could well be true and, if so, the preachers should do something about it, for sermons that fail to apply God's Word to the lives of the congregation fall far short of true preaching. But it may be that such a complaint merely reveals that the people concerned have never learned to think for themselves. Because of this they do not know how to apply the great principles of Scripture to particular areas in their lives, and so they have to be spoon-fed, like infants. There is a real danger of listening to sermons only to obtain spiritual aspirins for a particular problem, instead of learning from them the great truths that we can ourselves apply to any problem.

The Bible is not a long list of dos and don'ts; rather it contains principles that touch every aspect of life. For instance, the Bible says nothing about how many hours a week a Christian should spend watching television, but it says a great deal about the wise and proper use of time. It does not say how often a Christian should change his car, or how many suits or pairs of shoes he should have, but it says a great deal about the stewardship of our money. We shall never know spiritual stability unless we learn to apply the truths and principles of Scripture to everyday living. If you are to live like a Christian, then you must learn to think like a Christian. And you will never think like a Christian unless you spend more time with Christ. That means spending more time in prayer and Bible study.

Effective advance

If you have stability without mobility you will be like a lamppost—stable but cold; a lifeless pillar of concrete giving out light, but only in a very limited area. We need mobility so that the truth we know and love can move effectively against the enemy. The church of Christ needs to advance into battle. Rather than merely waiting to be attacked, it should be moving forward, taking the initiative and showing that its message is relevant to today's people. How do we make the gospel relevant? We do not *make* it so; it *is* relevant. As we let the gospel work out in our lives, the peace of God is seen and is brought to bear on a lost world.

Our lives, then, must bear evidence of this inward peace. The gospel of peace should produce in us an attitude of mind that sends us forward to face the foe, strong and confident in the Lord.

- Read Hebrews 13:20-21. It is a poor and pathetic soldier in the army of God who is not equipped with the knowledge of the God of peace.

- Read Philippians 4:6-7. You cannot fight if your mind is

50

filled with anxieties. The inward peace of God guards against outward cares and worries.

- Read Colossians 3:13-17. It is only when the peace of God reigns in the heart that we are fully equipped for battle.

A lethargic, unenthusiastic Christian is a denial of the New Testament faith. When our feet are shod as Paul advises, we can move into action with zeal and complete readiness. Zeal is not simply a matter of temperament; it is a product of the work of the gospel in the heart. If we have tasted of the gospel of peace and seen the invincible advantages it gives us, then with the gospel shoes on our feet we do not wait to be attacked, but rather we fly into battle.

At the end of the Second World War in 1945, nearly every commodity was scarce in Britain, and the people had to use ration books to obtain food, clothing and furniture. It was impossible to buy gym-shoes, but the schools had some for the children to use. It was a great day when the children were allowed to put on these very special shoes for PE or games lessons. The school yard would be filled with boys and girls running up and down in wild abandon. The zeal and enthusiasm this footwear gave them was unbelievable!

In the same way, when the Christian has his feet fitted with the gospel of peace, he will be ready and anxious to do battle in the name of his God and Saviour.

Put it on
This footwear is put on when the peace of God rules in our heart, and when our confidence rests unwaveringly on the truth of the gospel. We know then that we really are on the victory side.

7
The shield of faith

*'In addition to all this, take up the shield of faith,
with which you can extinguish all the flaming
arrows of the evil one.'*
(Ephesians 6:16)

The opening phrase of verse 16, 'In addition to all this', once more reminds us that we need the *full* armour of God. The belt, breastplate and shoes are vital, but they are not enough. So God provides three other pieces of equipment. The first three pieces are to be worn on the body: the second three we are told to 'take'.

The first three portions are more or less passive and preparatory; the soldier puts them on and keeps them on. But when you come to the second group there is a suggestion immediately of activity. The soldier may be sitting down in his room in the barracks and taking a period of rest, but he still keeps on his girdle of truth, his breastplate and his sandals. Then suddenly an alarm is given that the enemy is already attacking, and he immediately takes hold of his shield and his sword and puts on his helmet and rushes out. There is the suggestion of activity, of an actual fight and battle. You do not have the shield in your hand when you are resting; you put it down, and likewise your sword. But the moment the enemy becomes active again and there is an engagement, you have to take up these things in order that you may be ready for the conflict.

D. M. Lloyd-Jones

The Roman soldier's shield was very large. It was oblong in shape, almost like a door. Measuring 1.3m x 0.75m, it was made of wood and had its surface covered with a leather or metal lining which acted as a fire-proof defence against the enemy's 'flaming arrows'. These arrows were deadly, having metal tips wrapped round with an inflammable material, which was set alight before they were hurled at the foe. They were designed not only to penetrate, but also to burn and cause terrible injury. Against arrows like these the shield was the only adequate defence.

Flaming arrows

In the spiritual warfare our enemy the devil often hurls flaming arrows at us. We must never forget the truth of verse 12, that our struggle is not against flesh and blood, but against Satan and the powers of darkness. Satan will use men and women to attack us; but the most difficult times in the battle are not when we have to face the criticism of people or even the persecution of enemies. To a measure we can understand these things and cope with them. The real problems are the direct satanic assaults upon our minds and consciences. When Paul describes these assaults as 'flaming arrows', he is not just using picturesque language. It is a very accurate description.

As burning arrows not only pierced but set on fire what they pierced, they were doubly dangerous. They serve here therefore as the symbol of the fierce onsets of Satan. He showers arrows of fire on the soul of the believer; who, if

53

unprotected by the shield of faith, would soon perish. It is a common experience of the people of God that at times horrible thoughts, unholy, blasphemous, sceptical, malignant, crowd upon the mind, which cannot be accounted for on any ordinary law of mental action, and which cannot be dislodged. They stick like burning arrows; and fill the soul with agony. They can be quenched only by faith; by calling on Christ for help. These, however, are not the only kind of fiery darts; nor are they the most dangerous. There are others which enkindle passion, inflame ambition, excite cupidity [greed for gain], pride, discontent, or vanity; producing a flame which our deceitful heart is not so prompt to extinguish, and which is often allowed to burn until it produces great injury and even destruction. Against these most dangerous weapons of the evil one, the only protection is faith.

Charles Hodge

All Christians experience these attacks, whether they have recently been saved or whether they have been believers for fifty years. We pointed earlier to the stability and strength of Martin Luther, but even he was not immune from these flaming arrows. There is a famous story of him that one day he was so aware of the presence of the devil in his room that he threw his inkpot at the evil one!

Notice that these arrows are shot *at* us; therefore they do not originate from within us. It is very important for us to remember this, because one of the main intentions of the devil in using them is to bring us to despair. He wants us to believe that if we think and feel in this way, then we cannot possibly be Christians.

These arrows may take many forms. Sometimes they come when we are trying to read the Bible, and our concentration goes. Often in prayer our minds wander to all sorts of subjects, and the same thing can happen when we are listening to a sermon. These are satanic assaults; arrows shot into our minds to prevent us benefiting from the Scriptures and from prayer. By far the worst, however, are those evil thoughts that come to us —thoughts we would be deeply ashamed for anyone else to know about.

> The devil has often plagued some of the noblest saints with blasphemous thoughts—blasphemous thoughts about God, blasphemous thoughts about the Lord Jesus Christ. Horrible, horrifying! And . . . what the devil hopes and trusts will happen, is that the saint under attack will assume that they are his own thoughts and begin to doubt whether he is a Christian at all. Or the devil may hurl words and phrases, oaths, horrible language, at the Christian. His mind may appear to be filled with these. But none of them arise from the believer himself. They come from the devil who is trying to shake him, trying to confuse him, trying to persuade him that he is not a Christian, and that he has never been a Christian.
>
> *D. M. Lloyd-Jones*

The shield

The only answer to these assaults is the shield of faith. 'Your enemy the devil prowls around like a roaring lion looking for someone to devour. Resist him, standing firm in the faith, because you know that your brothers throughout the world are undergoing the same kind of sufferings' (1 Peter 5:8-9).

How do we hold up the shield of faith? By quietly applying what we know and believe of the grace of God, so as to divert all the enemy's arrows. It is the application of the other pieces of the armour to the particular danger. Suddenly you are under attack. You must stand firm and respond quickly (the shoes), by applying the truth (the belt), and trusting solely upon the righteousness of Christ (the breastplate).

Faith obviously includes what we believe, but it is more than that. Faith always acts, and its prime action is to point away from self to the love and grace of Almighty God.

Satan's plan is to get us looking at ourselves all the time. Sometimes we like what we see. We think we are quite good Christians, and certainly better than most; after all, we tithe our money and we never miss a prayer meeting . . . This means that the arrow of pride has found its mark. At other times (and perhaps more often) it is quite the opposite. We find prayer so difficult and the Christian life such a struggle that we begin to wonder if we really are Christians. The arrows of doubt and despair have struck home. God's remedy to both these problems is the shield of faith.

Remember that faith is not a noble quality found only in superior men. It is not a virtue attainable by a limited few. It is not the ability to persuade ourselves that black is white or that something we desire will come to pass if we only wish hard enough. Faith is simply the bringing of our minds into accord with the truth. It is adjusting our expectations to the promises of God in complete assurance that the God of the whole earth cannot lie.

A. W. Tozer

Faith will always point us to God and his promises. Read, in Romans 4:18-21, Paul's description of true faith in the life of Abraham. He was strengthened in his faith by believing the promise of God and giving glory to God. In other words, his eyes were fixed not upon himself, his strength or weaknesses, but upon his God. The Lord told him, 'Do not be afraid, Abram. I am your shield' (Genesis 15:1). Abraham believed that. Faith reminded him of the promise and caused him to trust the promiser. God makes similar promises to all his people.

We read in Psalm 3 of David being under attack. Many foes were against him, and they were saying that God would not help him. David knew better: 'But you are a shield around me, O LORD' (verse 3). He makes the same declaration in Psalm 28:7—The LORD is my strength and my shield; my heart trusts in him, and I am helped.' We too can have the same confidence, because the LORD 'is a shield to those who take refuge in him' (Proverbs 30:5). The Roman soldier hid behind his shield in the battle, and we too are to hide behind our shield, which is faith in the power and promises of the Lord.

The mind

These flaming arrows do not originate in us. They are shot at us by our enemy, and the main target is our mind. If the devil can affect the way we think, then he will triumph. Everything we do is controlled by our mind. Before our lips lie or gossip, our mind has given birth to the thoughts.

We need to be on our guard here, because at times we can allow ourselves to get into situations where sin is inevitable. If you read a certain type of book, full of sex and swearing, or if you watch certain television programmes, then this will affect your thinking. The cause of this is not the flaming arrows of the devil, but our own wilful disobedience; and the remedy is not the shield of faith, but repentance and obedience to the will of God.

But in either situation the mind is under attack, and therefore it is not surprising to find that the New Testament has a great deal to say about the Christian's mind and thinking:

'Do not conform any longer to the pattern of this world, but be transformed by the renewing of your mind. Then you will be able to test and approve what God's will is—his good, pleasing and perfect will' (Romans 12:2).

'Those who live according to the sinful nature have their minds set on what that nature desires; but those who live in accordance with the Spirit have their minds set on what the Spirit desires. The mind of sinful man is death, but the mind controlled by the Spirit is life and peace, because the sinful mind is hostile to God. It does not submit to God's law, nor can it do so. Those controlled by the sinful nature cannot please God' (Romans 8:5-8).

'Finally, brothers, whatever is true, whatever is noble, whatever is right, whatever is pure, whatever is lovely, whatever is admirable—if anything is excellent or praiseworthy—think abut such things. Whatever you have learned or received or heard from me, or seen in me—put it into practice. And the God of peace will be with you' (Philippians 4:8-9).

We have already seen that the only way to live like a Christian is to think like a Christian. And the only way to think like a Christian is to spend more time with Christ in prayer and Bible study. If our minds are full of Christ, then the flaming arrows will be able to do little damage.

Take up
We take up the shield of faith, not by trying to work up some sort of spiritual feeling, but by fleeing to God when the devil

attacks. Faith always leads straight to God. But faith needs to be nurtured and fed, and this is accomplished only in the presence of our Lord.

Habitual lively faith in Christ's presence and readiness to help is the secret of the Christian soldier fighting success-fully. It must never be forgotten that faith admits of degrees. All men do not believe alike, and even the same person has his ebbs and flows of faith, and believes more heartily at one time than another. According to the degree of his faith the Christian fights well or ill, wins victories, or suffers occasional repulses, comes off triumphant, or loses a battle. He that has most faith will always be the happiest and most comfortable soldier. Nothing makes the anxieties of warfare sit so lightly on a man as the assurance of Christ's love and continual protection. Nothing enables him to bear the fatigue of watching, struggling, and wrestling against sin, like the indwelling confidence that Christ is on his side and success is sure.

J. C. Ryle

8
The helmet of salvation

'Take the helmet of salvation.'
(Ephesians 6:17)

The purpose of the helmet is obviously to protect the soldier's head. Thus Paul draws attention to the need in the spiritual battle for the protection of our brain, understanding and thinking. We have already dealt briefly with the need to safeguard our thinking from the enemy's attacks, and this is a point that can never be too strongly emphasised. Here we shall focus particularly on the area of the Christian's understanding and attitude.

It is possible for you to believe all the correct doctrines, and to be able to use and apply them in such a way that you can skilfully pick up the shield of faith and deal with the devil's flaming arrows. In this way you can go on fairly satisfactorily in the Christian life. But after a while you grow tired and weary, and the battle begins to get you down. Then you begin to wonder, What is this all about? Is it worth the struggle? Am I taking Christianity too seriously? Am I spending too much time in church and on spiritual matters? Perhaps I ought to find some other interests. Perhaps I ought to pack in Christianity altogether.

Or it may happen in another way. You look outside of yourself, and you feel that Christianity is making so little impact. Perhaps you are in a small fellowship, with few Christian friends of your own age. Then you look at the world scene and hear news of Catholics and Protestants in conflict with each other in Northern Ireland, of Muslims and Christians fighting in Kosovo. And as you dwell on these things, you conclude that religion is a waste of time, nothing but hypocrisy.

Whichever form this takes, it is the devil who is attacking your understanding and attitude to life. How are we to deal with these assaults? We must learn from the many examples we find in the Scriptures.

Discouraged Hebrew Christians

The Epistle to the Hebrews was written to Jews who had been converted to Christianity. They were born-again believers, but they were facing extremely difficult times. Their fellow Jews regarded them as traitors and persecuted them bitterly. Some were stoned to death, and they faced problems unknown to Gentile Christians.

> Hitherto they had enjoyed the privileges of devout Israelites: they could take part in the beautiful and God-appointed services of the sanctuary; but now they were treated as unclean and apostates. Unless they gave up faith in Jesus, and forsook the assembling of themselves together, they were not allowed to enter the Temple, they were banished from the altar, the sacrifice, the high priest, the house of Jehovah.
>
> We can scarcely realize the piercing sword which thus wounded their inmost heart. That by clinging to the Messiah they were to be severed from Messiah's people, was, indeed, a great and perplexing trial; that for the hope of Israel's glory they were banished from the place which God had chosen, and where the divine Presence was

61

revealed, and the symbols and ordinances had been the joy and strength of their fathers; that they were to be no longer children of the covenant and of the house, but worse than Gentiles, excluded from the outer court, cut off from the commonwealth of Israel. This was indeed a sore and mysterious trial.

Adolph Saphir

The result of this was that they became very discouraged. Was it really worth it? They began to yearn for the old ceremonies, and particularly for the ministry of the high priest on their behalf. They had been expecting the Lord Jesus to come again in glory, but that had not materialised. The whole thing seemed to be going sour. Perhaps they would be better off if they gave up Christianity and returned to the Jewish fold.

God's remedy for that sort of thinking was the helmet of salvation. In other words, he reminds them throughout the epistle of the superiority of Christ.

A disillusioned psalmist

Psalm 73 reveals to us a man of God in a similar situation. His faith had almost gone because he had started looking at unbelievers and envying them (verses 2-3). They seemed to have everything easy (verses 4-5). They lived in wilful sin and got away with it (verses 6-12). His conclusion was that he was wasting his time trying to live for God (verses 13-14).

Once again we see the devil at work, attacking his understanding. 'When I tried to understand all this, it was oppressive to me' (verse 16). The answer was only found when he began to consider the ways and purposes of God (verses 17-28).

Whether it is a discouraged Christian or a disillusioned psalmist, the problem is the same:

The devil succeeds at times in persuading us to become so

preoccupied with the details of the Christian life that we forget the grand truth covering the whole. We are so concerned about the trees that we miss the wood; we are so immersed in the local tactics that we forget the great campaign. 'The world is too much with us.' We are so keenly aware of the heat and the burden of the day that we forget who we are, we forget what we are destined for. The result of all this, of course, is that we begin to feel that we cannot go on, that it is too much for us. 'The struggle naught availeth.' Our wounds are all in vain, and all our labour is in vain. The devil, we feel, is too strong, too subtle for us; he is sure to defeat us.

D. M. Lloyd-Jones

The helmet

In what way does salvation act as a helmet in warding off this particular type of assault? Does 'the helmet of salvation' mean an awareness of our salvation? Are we to remember that, because we are saved, we can face even the most terrible of enemies and not only survive, but confidently expect to triumph? This is certainly part of it, but there is more to it than that. We discover the full meaning in 1 Thessalonians 5:8 — 'But since we belong to the day, let us be self-controlled, putting on faith and love as a breastplate, and the *hope of salvation* as a helmet.'

In the New Testament the word 'hope' always points to the future, and it always means full and complete assurance. There is nothing uncertain about Christian hope. It is because we are saved now, that we have the certain hope that not only shall we always be saved, but our salvation will be even more glorious when the Lord Jesus Christ comes again for his redeemed. Then our salvation will be final and complete: we

63

shall be free not only from the guilt and consequence of sin, but also from its power and influence.

So when the devil comes to distort our understanding and depress us with thoughts of giving up the fight, we are to put on the helmet of the hope of salvation. We look past the present difficulties to the future glory. The cynic will argue that that is 'pie in the sky when you die'. Not so. There is a present glory and joy in being a Christian. The discouragement is not the norm but the exception. Still, it can cause serious problems, and we need to remind ourselves that 'our present sufferings are not worth comparing with the glory that will be revealed in us' (Romans 8:18). This is the helmet, the hope of glory.

There is a clear example of this in Christ's teaching in Matthew 24. The description he gives of 'the end of the age' is awesome and frightening (verses 6-11). The devil will be quick to take advantage of the situation to attack the thinking and understanding of believers, and as a result 'the love of most will grow cold' (verse 12). But Jesus says we are to 'stand firm' (verse 13). How is it possible to stand firm in the face of such attacks on our faith? The answer is in verses 30 and 31: it is the hope—that is, the absolute certainty—that our Saviour will come for us.

The same perspective is seen in 2 Corinthians 4. In verse 6 we have a thrilling declaration of what happened when we were saved: 'God . . . made his light shine in our hearts . . .' Then immediately following this we are faced with a description of severe problems. These are the problems of a man whose dark heart has been illuminated by 'the light of the knowledge of the glory of God in the face of Christ'. How is the man to cope with them? The answer is in verse 14: we know—here is absolute certainty yet again—of the hope of glory. Because of this Paul goes on to say: 'Therefore we do not lose heart . . . For our light and momentary troubles are achieving for us an eternal glory that far outweighs them all. So we fix our eyes not on what is seen, but on what is unseen. For what is seen is temporary, but what is unseen is eternal' (verses 16-18).

Put it on

This is the way to put on the helmet of salvation: fix your eyes on the future glory, and rejoice in it. How can we lose heart and give in, with such a prospect before us?

This then is the meaning of the helmet of salvation. You are tempted, discouraged, disillusioned and weary of the battle. Your mind fills with doubts and despair. Give it all up, says the enemy. You answer, I know it is difficult, but I am saved and I have a great hope of salvation. At that point you are beginning to get things back into perspective. You are fixing your eyes on the unseen but sure and blessed hope.

> *Stand up, stand up for Jesus!*
> *The strife will not be long;*
> *This day the noise of battle,*
> *The next the victor's song.*
> *To him that overcometh*
> *A crown of life shall be;*
> *He with the King of glory*
> *Shall reign eternally.*
>
> George Duffield

9
The sword of the Spirit

'Take . . . the sword of the Spirit,
which is the word of God.'
(Ephesians 6:17)

The last piece of the armour is, strictly speaking, not part of the armour at all. Each of the other pieces is designed to protect a particular part of the body; they are all defensive. The sword, however, does not protect a particular part, but the whole of the body; and it protects not by deadening a blow but by holding the enemy back. In addition, it is not merely defensive, but very much an offensive weapon; it can destroy the enemy.

Paul calls it 'the sword of the Spirit', and then, to make absolutely sure that we know what he means, he adds, 'which is the word of God'. This sword, the only weapon of attack in our fight against Satan, is provided by the Holy Spirit, and it is the inspired, infallible, inerrant Word of God. The Bible is crucial in the spiritual battle. We do not fight in our own strength, neither do we fight with our own weapons. Our own ideas and thoughts will be useless, but the Scriptures are part of the mighty power of God (verse 10). 'The weapons we fight with are not the weapons of the world. On the contrary, they have divine power to demolish strongholds' (2 Corinthians 10:4).

It [the Word of God] has the power not only of truth, but of divine truth. Our Lord promised to give to His disciples a

66

word and wisdom which all their adversaries should not be able to gainsay or resist. In opposition to all error, to all false philosophy, to all false principles of morals, to all the sophistries of vice, to all the suggestions of the devil, the sole, simple, and sufficient answer is the Word of God. This puts to flight all the powers of darkness. The Christian finds this to be true in his individual experience. It dissipates his doubts; it drives away his fears; it delivers him from the power of Satan. It is also the experience of the church collective. All her triumphs over sin and error have been effected by the Word of God. So long as she uses this and relies on it alone, she goes on conquering; but when any thing else, be it reason, science, tradition, or the commandments of men, is allowed to take its place or to share its office, then the church, or the Christian, is at the mercy of the adversary.

Charles Hodge

We have already seen that the Bible is the truth of God, and that it is reliable and authoritative (2 Peter 1:20-21; 2 Timothy 3:16). It is the best weapon possible, and is more powerful than any gun, bomb or missile. The balance of power in the spiritual warfare is always firmly on the side of the Christian, because the weapon God provides for him is far superior to anything the enemy has. If he knows how to use the sword of the Spirit, the Christian need never be 'outgunned'. But to have the sword is one thing: to be skilled in its use is another. Just as the Bible is provided by the Holy Spirit, so it is only the Holy Spirit who can help us use it effectively.

Understanding

Before you can use Scripture, you must understand it; and before you will understand it, you must believe it is worth understanding. If you do not, you will not take the time and effort to study it, and there is no understanding without study. Bible study is not merely an intellectual exercise. It is something unique. There are many books on a variety of subjects that you will probably never be able to understand; you may not have the intellect or ability to do so. But because you are a Christian, and therefore indwelt by the Holy Spirit, you can understand the Word of God. Read 1 Corinthians 2:6-16. The Christian can understand because we have received 'the Spirit who is from God, that we may understand what God has freely given us' (verse 12).

As in any battle, the enemy seeks to destroy or nullify our armaments. We have seen how the devil has strenuously sought to undermine the truth and reliability of the Bible, but he does not stop there. He causes some believers to think that, because they are not very well educated, they cannot expect to understand the more difficult teachings of Scripture. That is a lie. Never forget that the Epistle to the Romans, which contains some of the most involved doctrinal teaching in the Bible, was written not to university graduates at Rome, but to the church there, a church which was made up of very ordinary people, many of them slaves. Paul never thought his writings would be too difficult. He knew that minds enlightened by the Holy Spirit would be able to understand, if they really wanted to.

For many centuries Satan used the Roman Catholic Church to keep the Bible from ordinary people. They were forbidden to have a copy, and if they did, they could not read it because it was in Latin. Translations into the language of the people were sought out and burnt. Men like William Tyndale gave their lives so that we could have the Bible in English. The Protestant Reformation was used by God to give the people the Bible in their own language so that they could understand his divine ways. The Reformers taught the Scriptures, but were well aware of the necessity of the Holy Spirit's enlightenment.

> We ought not to measure, censure and understand the Scriptures according to our own natural sense and reason, but we ought diligently by prayer to meditate therein and to search after the same. The Holy Ghost must be the only master to teach us, and let youth and scholar not be ashamed to learn of this tutor.
>
> *Martin Luther*

> For as God alone can properly bear witness to his own words, so these words will not obtain full credit in the hearts of men, until they are sealed by the inward testimony of the Spirit.
>
> *John Calvin*

An open Bible

So you open the Bible and begin to read. As you do so, remember what you are reading. It is not a novel, not a biography, not a newspaper; it is God's Word, the Holy Bible. Therefore come to it with a serious and earnest mind. And before you come, pray and ask God the Holy Spirit to give you understanding. 'Open my eyes that I may see wonderful things in your law' (Psalm 119:18).

The Bible is a unique book, and one of its unique features is that you do not start reading at the beginning. Do not start in Genesis. You need to understand something of the New Testament before the Old Testament will appear relevant to you. Start in the Gospels—read them all. Then go over Mark's Gospel more slowly, using the notes contained in *Read, Mark, Learn* by John Blanchard (available from any Christian bookshop). Then, for a general introduction to the whole Bible, use the notes in *Firm Foundations*, written by Peter Jeffery and Owen Milton.

When should you read the Bible? Daily. There is no question about this. It must be daily for two basic reasons:

- 'Man does not live on bread alone, but on every word that comes from the mouth of God' (Matthew 4:4). The great general Napoleon believed that an army marches on its stomach. He meant that good food every day was essential for the efficiency and success of his soldiers. As soldiers of the Lord, we need daily spiritual food to strengthen us for the battle.
- The Word of God is like a vast reservoir. Its provisions can never be exhausted. We need to study it daily if we are to get anywhere near a grasp and understanding of its teaching.

Make your daily time in God's Word precious to your soul. Neglect it for nothing.

Purpose

Let us remind ourselves of the reason why we read the Bible. We are soldiers in a battle, and our purpose is to train ourselves in the use of our only weapon, the sword of the Spirit. Knowledge and understanding of Scripture will do certain necessary things for us.

It will enable us to grow	1 Peter 2:2
It will gain God's approval	2 Timothy 2:15
It is superb training	2 Timothy 3:16-17
It helps us overcome sin	Psalm 119:9-11
It is the only way to success	Joshua 1:7-8

So you see how vital the Bible is to a Christian. Daily devotions and daily training are crucial. Reading the Bible, studying it, meditating on its teaching—these are the only ways to be skilled soldiers who can effectively use the sword of the Spirit.

Failure

What happens if a Christian fails to give sufficient time and effort to the Word, and therefore never really understands it? This is not a hypothetical question; it all too often happens. To answer it, let us ask another in line with Paul's illustration of the Roman soldier. What would happen if a soldier went into battle without his sword? He would be easy to defeat. He would offer no threat to the enemy, and he would also be a liability to his own side. His comrades would not be able to rely upon him and would have to spend a lot of time rescuing him.

If we do not understand the Bible, certain things will follow inevitably. We cannot obey what we do not know. Ignorance is the great enemy of truth. In the Christian life it is possible to do many sinful things simply because we do not know what God has to say about them. This will lead to a lack of spiritual growth. And if you do not grow and become stronger in the faith, you cannot take your fair share of responsibility in the battle. You become a liability and a brake on the progress of the church. Read Hebrews 5:11-14.

So then, if we are to avoid failure, we must know and understand the Bible, and understand all of it, not merely a set of proof texts. There is great value in memorising Scripture, but beware of just learning a list of proof texts. The danger of this is that you tend to think of a particular subject or doctrine only in terms of the verse memorised, forgetting that Scripture has a lot more than this to say on most subjects. Make it your ambition to know *all* the Word. This will take time, but it is very rewarding. And never forget that rightly understanding the Bible is not a mechanical process. The Word of God has to be spiritually understood. It is the sword of the Spirit, and the Holy Spirit is the best instructor.

Skilful use

The purpose of understanding the Bible is not to pass examinations, nor to show people how clever we are; it is to use the sword against sin. How do we do this? The Holy Spirit shows us in the Scriptures. There are several examples, the classic one being in Luke 4:1-12. Here we have the account of Jesus being tempted by the devil. Notice that each temptation was answered with a quotation from the Old Testament book of Deuteronomy (Luke 4:4, 8, 12). Jesus did not discuss or argue; he used the sword. If the eternal Son of God needs to use Scripture like this, how much more do we! In times of temptation the Word of God is always the greatest defence and argument.

> Let us learn from this single fact, if we learn nothing else from this wondrous history, the high authority of the Bible, and the immense value of a knowledge of its contents. Let us read it, search into it, pray over it, diligently, perseveringly, unweariedly. Let us strive to be so thoroughly acquainted with its pages, that its texts may abide in our memories, and stand ready at our right hand in the day of need. Let us be able to appeal from every perversion and false interpretation of its meaning, to those thousand plain passages, which are written as it were with a sunbeam. The Bible is indeed a sword, but we must take heed that we know it well, if we would use it with effect.
>
> *J. C. Ryle*

We often need to ask ourselves questions like these: What is right or wrong? Shall I do it or not? Shall I go there or not? The answer is always to be found in the Bible: not in long lists of dos and don'ts, but in principles that cover every possible situation. Using the sword is not just a matter of quoting a few odd verses; it is knowing the Word and being able to apply it to every eventuality. In Luke 4:10 the devil quotes Scripture (Psalm 91:11-12), but his use of it is entirely wrong. Jesus is not taken in by the fact that these words come out of the Bible. Because he knows the Bible, he is aware of what is happening, and in verse 12 he answers, 'Do not put the Lord your God to the test' (Deuteronomy 6:16). This point is particularly important when the devil sends a Mormon or Jehovah's Witness to knock on your door. They quote from the Bible, but they always either twist its meaning or quote out of context. And, by the way, they also carefully ignore a lot of Scripture.

Of course, it is not only in temptation that we need to use the sword. It is a weapon of attack as well as defence. We are to attack Satan and carry the fight into his strongholds of darkness. Therefore in witness and evangelism the sword of the Spirit must be to the forefront. When Jesus has to deal with an enquiring soul in Mark 10, he used the sword. In answer to the question, 'What must I do to inherit eternal life?' (verse 17), Jesus quoted the Ten Commandments in order to show the young man what sin is. Note that Jesus used the Law, not merely a collection of gospel texts. This is skilful use of the sword—the right verses at the right time. When we see the apostles evangelising in the book of Acts, they are always using the sword. Read Peter's famous sermon in Acts 2, and notice how much of it is direct application of Scripture. Paul does the same thing (Acts 17:2). Witnessing is not merely a matter of giving a testimony; it is telling sinners what God has to say about them. It is using the sword of the Spirit.

There is no substitute for the sword of the Spirit, which is the Word of God. We must never try to separate the Word and the Spirit. The Holy Spirit will never speak contrary to the Word. He never bypasses Scripture. But the Word without the Spirit is meaningless. The Spirit uses the Word and 'the Spirit gives life'. So, love the Word, care for it, read it, know it, and then use it. With it resist the devil, and he will flee from you.

10
'Each piece put on
with prayer'

*'And pray in the Spirit on all occasions with all kinds of
prayers and requests. With this in mind, be alert and
always keep on praying for all the saints.'*
(Ephesians 6:18)

Paul has concluded his teaching on the armour of God. Taking the analogy of the Roman soldier, he has looked at the various pieces of the soldier's armour and illustrated from them the armour the Christian needs as he fights the devil. In doing so, he has drawn out vital spiritual lessons. One is that the full armour of God is essential. It is no use going into battle with half the armour on, and the other half ignored. God's provision for us is complete, and we need it all. Then, secondly, God provides the armour for us, but we must put it on. This involves discipline and effort. We are not merely to admire it; we are not simply to get out the Brasso every now and again and polish it up: we are to put it on. It is not ornamental, but something very serviceable.

We have examined what each piece means, and I trust that by now we understand their importance. So we clothe ourselves with this armour. Each day very carefully we put on the helmet of salvation and the breastplate of righteousness and the rest of God's provision. We are ready now for the battle, and it is not very long before Satan's flaming arrows and other evil assaults come our way. We are confident in God's armour, but yet we find ourselves defeated once again. Why is this? Is it that the armour is useless? No, the problem is not with the armour. The problem is *how* we put the armour on. The reason for defeat is lack of prayer. The hymn-writer was perfectly correct when he wrote:

> *Put on the gospel armour,*
> *Each piece put on with prayer.*

Paul's teaching on the armour of God does not finish with verse 17; he immediately goes on to show us how vital prayer is in the battle. Even though prayer is not a part of the armour, it is indispensable to the success of the armour.

This means, then, that the armour which is provided for us by God cannot be used except in fellowship and communion with God. The armour God provides for us must never be thought of mechanically, still less magically. The danger, the temptation, is to feel that as long as we put on this armour there is no more to be done; all is well, the armour will in and of itself protect us, and do so mechanically. So having put it on, we can relax, and put watching aside. But that is the exact opposite of the true position, says the Apostle; to think in that way means that you are already defeated. The armour, and the spiritual application of it, must always be conceived of in a vital and in a living manner. Every single piece, excellent thought it is in itself, will not suffice us, and will not avail us, unless always and at all times we are in a living relationship to God and receiving strength and power from him.

D. M. Lloyd-Jones

Strength and power

What the armour represents—imputed righteousness, the hope of salvation, etc.—is great and glorious, but these things in and of themselves are not enough. We need strength and power to wear the armour, and that is only found in communion and fellowship with God, which, in turn, means prayer. You could saddle up a horse, strap a suit of armour to it and send it into battle. The armour is there in its completeness, but it will be useless. It is just an empty shell. We may as well not put on the armour at all, if we think that God merely hands it out like some divine quartermaster in the sky. Our God is not like that, neither is he like a car-hire firm merely providing a service. God does not hire his armour out, because without him it would be useless. In other words, Paul is telling us that we need the strength of God himself to fight this battle, not merely the equipment he provides.

We must and ought to praise God for each piece of the armour. They are all indispensable, but we need more than these. When Paul introduces the subject of prayer, he is in effect only repeating what he has said in verse 10: 'Finally, be strong in the Lord and in his mighty power.' The word 'finally' tells us that everything that follows is only an elaboration of that. Putting on the full armour, together with prayer, is how we are able to 'be strong in the Lord and in his mighty power'. We need to maintain personal, intimate fellowship with our heavenly Father and, for this, prayer is essential.

In the Christian life there is always a potential danger of becoming spiritually unbalanced. There are believers who really know the Scriptures, but in the battle they are useless. They cannot apply the truth either in their own lives in sanctification or to unbelievers in evangelism. They know the truth, but there is no power, no life behind it. The reason invariably is a neglect of prayer. On the other hand, there are believers who spend hours in prayer, and they are also useless in the battle, because of ignorance of God's revealed truth.

Strength and power come from putting on the whole armour and infusing it with the life that comes only from prayer communion with Almighty God.

> Prayer must buckle on all the other parts of our Christian armour, v.18. We must join prayer with all these graces, for our defence against these spiritual enemies, imploring help and assistance of God, as the case requires: and we must pray always.
>
> *Matthew Henry*

For an explanation of 'praying in the Spirit', and 'all kinds of prayer', it would be helpful to read the chapter on 'Prayer' in another publication in this series, called *Walk Worthy*. As breath is to our body, so prayer is to our soul. We must pray all types of prayer, on all occasions, and above all we need to pray in the Spirit. So we must work at this, and if it is not true of us now, we must make sure that it becomes true. We must order our lives so that it becomes true. We must give time to prayer so that it is not fitted into a busy life, but is the centre of our life. Prayer is communion with God, and there is nothing more important than that. Everything pales into insignificance compared with this. If we do not have communion and fellowship with God, then we have nothing and we are nothing. But if we do, then we are strong; more than that, we are invincible.

Put on the full armour of God and pray. This will not make the battle any easier, but it will mean the difference between defeat and victory.

Stand, then, in his great might,
With all his strength endued;
And take, to arm you for the fight,
The panoply of God.
To keep your armour bright
Attend with constant care,
Still serving in your Captain's sight,
And watching unto prayer.

From strength to strength go on;
Wrestle and fight and pray;
Tread all the powers of darkness down,
And win the well-fought day;
That, having all things done,
And all your conflicts past,
Ye may o'ercome through Christ alone,
And stand complete at last.

Charles Wesley

11
Victory

*'But thanks be to God! He gives us the
victory through our Lord Jesus Christ.'*
(1 Corinthians 15:57)

The great thing about the spiritual battle is that the victory
is assured. The battle is between God and Satan. We are
involved because we are Christians, but it is not *our* battle; the
battle is the Lord's. Satan is a mighty being, but God is
almighty and invincible. This is why victory is assured. In
order to understand the nature of the victory, let us once again
examine the nature of the battle. To do so we will draw an
analogy between this and the battle for the Falklands in 1982.

On the Falkland Islands were living a community of men,
women and children in peace. They were under the rule and
protection of the British Crown, and they were happy to be so.
But all that changed when an enemy invaded, imposing upon
them a foreign rule and authority, and taking away their
freedom. So far as the Falkland islanders were concerned,
there was nothing they could do. They were too weak to resist,
and their only hope was that Britain would value them enough
to come to the rescue. This Britain did. Negotiations and talk
proved hopeless, so a task force was sent; the enemy must be
defeated and forced to withdraw. The cost of achieving this, in
terms of lives and equipment, was enormous. Some argued
that the price was too high and the Falklands were not worth

it. But the price was paid. Lives were lost, victory was accomplished, and when freedom was restored to the islanders there was great rejoicing. The enemy, however, though defeated and humiliated, did not relinquish its claims to the Falklands, and so the threat still hangs over the victors. As well as that, the enemy left behind many minefields and booby traps, and these will be a potential source of danger for a long time to come. Of the victory there is no doubt, but the threat and danger are still there.

The world is God's creation, and he put man and woman in it to enjoy its beauty and to live for his glory. It was under God's authority and rule. Then Satan invaded with his great weapon of sin. Adam and Eve were soon defeated, and ever since the whole of mankind has been enslaved. Satan rules as the prince of this world. So far as man was concerned there was nothing that could be done; indeed, unlike the Falkland islanders, man became a willing captive. Our only hope was that the Lord would value us enough to come to the rescue. This God did. There were no negotiations. Satan, the enemy, must be defeated and man set free. But God sent no task force bristling with armaments. Instead, 'God sent his Son, born of a woman, born under law, to redeem those under law, that we might receive the full rights of sons' (Galatians 4:4). The cost to God was enormous: his Son must die to redeem guilty sinners. It could well be argued that the price was too high, and that sinners are not worth it. But still the Lord paid the price. Jesus died on Calvary and the victory was accomplished.

Salvation has been purchased for us by the precious blood of Jesus, and souls rejoice when they are saved. But Satan, though defeated, does not give up, and he continues to threaten the redeemed. As well as that, he still exerts an influence, because our old sinful nature is not dead and it acts like a spiritual minefield. Of the victory there is no doubt, but the threat and danger are still there.

From this we can see that there are three different types of victory.

The victory of salvation

If you are a Christian this has taken place already. Without this victory you would know nothing of the battle. You would still be a prisoner of Satan, shut up in the dungeon of sin. When God in his love and mercy saves a soul it is a moment of great triumph. This is the fruit of Christ's great victory over the devil on the cross. The victory of salvation is the triumph over the guilt and condemnation of sin. At the moment of salvation, condemnation is replaced by justification. In other words, the guilty sinner is made right with God. We are acceptable to God because of the righteousness of Jesus. The law of God demands that the wages of sin, which is death, be paid out in full. Justification fully meets the rightful demands of the law by crediting us with the righteousness of Jesus (Romans 3:21-26). When Jesus died on the cross, he died in our place, as our substitute, bearing our sin and guilt (2 Corinthians 5:18-21).

The victory of salvation means:

no condemnation	Romans 8:1
forgiveness of sin	Ephesians 1:7
reconciliation	Colossians 1:21-22

That victory is absolute. Nothing can change it. It is a total victory because what Christ did on the cross for us was a perfect work of atonement. Therefore the salvation he gives us can never be taken from us (John 10:28-29). This, then, is a victory to rejoice over. The celebration of this victory should be a daily experience for Christians as we thank God for saving us.

The victory of the Christian life

Even though we have victory in the Lord Jesus Christ over the guilt and condemnation of sin, its evil power and influence daily threaten our peace with God. Our salvation cannot be lost, but the joy of it can depart, and so too can the assurance of it, unless we know victory in the Christian life over the power of sin. It is for this victory that we need the armour of God. We must never forget that we are only in the battle because the victory of salvation is a personal reality. The battle is evidence that we truly are Christians. But all too often we seem to experience not victory but defeat. We lose our temper, we become jealous, pride puffs us up, sin walks all over us. Defeat seems to be the norm in the Christian life, and victory a rarity.

However much this may seem to be the case, it is simply not true. This is one of the great tactics of Satan. It is true that we are not perfect, and never will be in this life; it is true that we are none of us what we ought to be as Christians; but, thank God, it is also true we are not what we once were. Examine yourself. Isn't this so? You are very aware of your sin (Satan will see to that), but are you not also aware of God's sanctifying work in you? You do not live and act as you used to do. You read the Bible and pray now; you never did that previously. Are there not a hundred and one little things that are evidence of victory over sin in your life? It may be a strange thing to say, but it is none the less true, that the more we are aware of Satan in our lives, the less influence he is having.

The battle is evidence of the power of sin, but the fact that you are still going on with the Lord is evidence of victory in many areas of your life. We do not want to be complacent and indifferent to the many defeats we suffer, but neither do we want to minimise the work of grace that is going on in us. We must groan in repentance before God for the times when temptation overcomes us, but we must also learn to rejoice and praise the Lord when his power enables us to be victorious over temptation.

When we clothe ourselves with the armour of God, and are able to stand firm and triumph over the assaults of Satan, then victory has indeed a sweet taste. It is not the taste of pride, but of humility, for we are aware that in our own strength we are hopeless. Our victory is only because of our relationship to the Lord Jesus Christ. Nevertheless, God wants us to rejoice in it and daily offer our thanks and praise to him who is 'of sin the double cure'—the blessed Lord Jesus who alone can 'cleanse me from its guilt and power'.

The final victory
The final victory is the complete eradication of sin, evil and ungodliness. This will take place when Jesus comes again into this world, not this time in humiliation but in glory, and Satan will be banished for ever. To grasp something of the wonder and completeness of this victory, read the following Scriptures:

The promise of the coming	John 14:1-4
It will be for believers	1 Thessalonians 4:13-18
It will be for judgement	Matthew 25:31-46
New heavens and new earth	2 Peter 3:1-13
The triumph of Christ	Revelation 19
The judgement of Satan	Revelation 20

84

The purpose of the battle is to defeat Satan, to restore God's glory unchallenged in this world, and to re-establish the whole of creation as it was before sin polluted its perfection. Christ's victory on the cross has gone a long way towards accomplishing this. For instance, we see in Genesis 3 that when Adam sinned, he lost certain privileges: he lost peace with God and became afraid of God (verse 10); he lost access into the presence of God and was banished (verses 23-24). Both these lost privileges are restored in salvation—read Romans 5:1-2. This is now our experience, because of Christ's victory on the cross and his victory in our lives. But still Satan's influence and sin's power are very evident in the world. This is not because God has failed to defeat him or that the cross was not a complete victory. It is the way that God has chosen to fight the battle and gain the victory.

There is no doubt about the final victory. The cross of Calvary and the empty tomb assure us of that. Satan is already a defeated foe. The final victory will be celebrated when God brings into being 'a new heaven and a new earth, the home of righteousness' (2 Peter 3:13).

When God made man, he first of all made a world for him to live in. Man was not made as a spirit; from the beginning he was made body, soul and spirit, and God made him to live in a physical universe. My argument is that, if God is to defeat Satan finally and completely, he must restore everything to its original condition. So if heaven just means those of us who are believers are finally going to get rid of this old body and dwell in a spiritual realm in a purely spiritual condition, then redemption and salvation are not complete. God's plan of redemption is not complete until there is an earth for man to live in and on, in the body.

85

Paradise regained cannot be anything less than that. Thank God, that is the very thing Scripture teaches. We are not to look forward merely to a vague, indefinite, nebulous spiritual state. No, we shall be in the body, and we shall be on a new earth, under new heavens, wherein dwelleth righteousness. That, and nothing short of that, will establish God's glory and his final triumph over the devil and all who belong to him.

D. M. Lloyd-Jones